6/08

Great Journeys Across Earth

AMUNDSEN AND SCOTT'S RACE TO THE SOUTH POLE

Liz Gogerly

Heinemann Library
Chicago, Illinois

© 2008 Heinemann Library
a division of Reed Elsevier Inc.
Chicago, Illinois

Customer Service 888-454-2279
Visit our website at www.heinemannraintree.com

Produced for Heinemann Library by
Monkey Puzzle Media Ltd.

Designed by Jane Hawkins and Victoria Bevan.

Originated by Modern Age.
Printed and bound in China

12 11 10 09 08
10 9 8 7 6 5 4 3 2 1

**Library of Congress Cataloging-in-Publication
Data**
Gogerly, Liz.
   Amundsen and Scott's race to the South Pole / Liz
Gogerly.
     p. cm. -- (Great journeys across Earth)
   Includes bibliographical references and index.
   ISBN-13: 978-1-4034-9753-6 (hb) --
   ISBN-13: 978-1-4034-9761-1 (pb)
1. Amundsen, Roald, 1872-1928--Travel--
Antarctica--Juvenile literature. 2. Scott, Robert
Falcon, 1868-1912--Travel--Antarctica--Juvenile
literature. 3. Antarctica--Discovery and exploration-
-Juvenile literature. 4. South Pole--Discovery and
exploration--Juvenile literature. I. Title.
G850 1912 .A48 G64 2007
919.8'9--dc22
                                  2007005829

Acknowledgments
The author and publisher are grateful to the
following for permission to reproduce copyright
material: Alamy p. **23** (Bernie Epstein); Corbis pp.
8 (Bettmann), **35** (Galen Rowell), **38–39** (Chris
Rainier); FLPA pp. **11** (Tui De Roy/Minden Pictures),
14 (David Hosking), **31** (Colin Monteath/Minden
Pictures); Getty Images pp. **1** (Hulton Archive),
9 (Hulton Archive), **13** (Gordon Wiltsie/National
Geographic), **21** (Time & Life), **28** (Roger Mear),
32 (Hulton Archive), **34** (Time & Life), **41** (National
Geographic); Mary Evans Picture Library pp. **5**,
16; MPM Images p. **33**; Nature Picture Library pp.
15 (Doug Allan), **16–17** (Eric Baccega), **19** (David
Tipling); Popperfoto.com p. **30**; Royal Geographical
Society pp. **7**, **12**, **25**; Science Photo Library p. **20**
(Doug Allan); Still Pictures p. **27** (Michael Graber);
Topfoto pp. **6** (HIP), **18**, **29**, **36** (Roger-Viollet), **37**.

Maps by Martin Darlison at Encompass Graphics.

Cover photograph of a gentoo penguin on the
Antarctic Peninsula reproduced with permission
of Alamy (Robert Harding Picture Library Ltd).

Title page photograph: Helmer Hanssen, one
of Roald Amundsen's party, poses at the South
Pole with the Norwegian flag.

Expert read by Dr. Paulette Posen, environmental
research scientist at the University of East Anglia,
United Kingdom.

Disclaimer
All the Internet addresses (URLs) given in this book
were valid at the time of going to press. However,
due to the dynamic nature of the Internet, some
addresses may have changed or ceased to exist
since publication. While the author and publishers
regret any inconvenience this may cause readers,
no responsibility for any such changes can be
accepted by either the author or the publishers.

Contents

Some words are shown in bold, **like this**. You can find out what they mean by looking in the glossary.

"Sorrowful Camp"

In November 1912 a group of men set off from their camp in icy Antarctica. They were looking for the British explorer Captain Robert Scott and his four companions. The men had been missing for eight long months.

Will they return?

Captain Scott and his team were due back at camp at the end of March 1912. Other members of their expedition waited as a freezing winter set in. They spent dark days and nights, hoping that Scott, Captain Lawrence Oates, Edgar Evans, Dr. Edward Wilson, and Lieutenant Henry Bowers might appear.

This map of Antarctica shows the position of the South Pole. The lines on the map show **latitude** and **longitude** (see page 12).

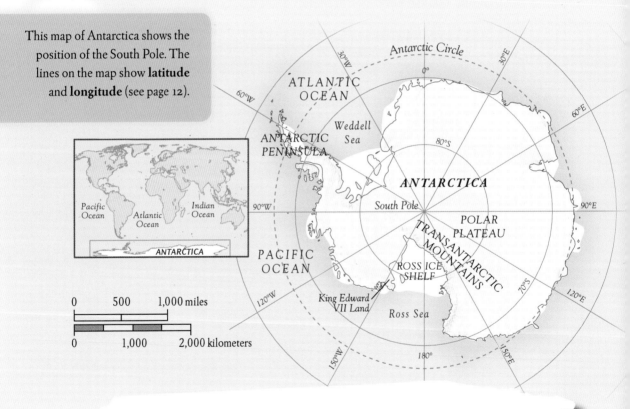

Antarctica facts
- *Antarctica is a continent surrounded by ocean. It lies at the far south of the globe, around the **South Pole**.*
- *Antarctica covers a massive 5,396,000 square miles (13,975,000 square kilometers), making it nearly twice the size of Australia.*
- *The South Polar ice sheet covers about 98 percent of Antarctica. In some places the ice sheet is 2.5 miles (4 kilometers) thick.*

Time passed slowly, but months later there was still no sign of the lost men. Eventually, winter ended and the weather improved enough for a search party to leave the camp.

On November 12 the searchers finally spotted something poking up out of the snow. They had stumbled upon a tent. Inside the tent they found Bowers and Wilson inside their sleeping bags. They seemed to have died peacefully in their sleep. The extreme cold had turned their skin yellow and glassy. Between the two men lay Captain Scott, half out of his sleeping bag. His face looked pained and was partly eaten away by **frostbite**.

What had brought Scott and his companions to this terrible, lonely death?

This painting shows the grave of Captain Scott and his companions. It marks the place where the tent was found.

"A ghastly sight"

Thomas Williamson, one of the searchers, described finding Robert Scott's tent:

"I shed a few tears and I know the others did the same. It came as a great shock although we knew we should meet this sort of thing. . . . I felt I could not look, but when at last I made up my mind I saw a ghastly sight. . . . Their sufferings must have been terrible. . . . We called the place Sorrowful Camp."

Journey to the South

Robert Scott had visited Antarctica once before the trip that led to his death. In 1899 he was chosen by Sir Clements Markham, president of the London **Royal Geographical Society**, to take a British expedition there.

First attempt

Sir Clements Markham said in 1895: "The exploration of the Antarctic regions is the greatest piece of geographical exploration yet to be undertaken." He trusted Scott as expedition leader, and they planned the trip together.

Scott set off in 1901 on board the ship *Discovery*. With his team, he explored the Ross Sea area (see map on page 4). He discovered King Edward VII Land and made the first balloon flight over Antarctica. Eventually, lack of food forced Scott's expedition to turn back. But he had still traveled 300 miles (483 kilometers) farther south than anyone else before.

Captain Robert Scott

Robert Falcon Scott (1868–1912) was born in Devonport, Devon, in southwest England. He joined the navy at the age of 18, and in 1897 was made a lieutenant on Majestic, one of the finest British warships of the time. Scott was 32 years old when Sir Clements Markham chose him to head the Discovery mission of 1901–1904. Afterwards Scott returned to the navy and became a captain. In 1908 he married the sculptor Kathleen Bruce. The couple had a son, named Peter, shortly before Scott set off for Antarctica again.

This portrait shows Captain Robert Falcon Scott in naval uniform. He was a fit, proud man with a strong personality.

Fresh challenge

The United States, France, Russia, Sweden, Germany, Great Britain, and Norway all made further attempts to explore Antarctica. However, by 1909 the **South Pole** had still not been reached. It remained a challenge. Who would claim the honor of being the first nation to go there? Captain Scott announced in September 1909 that he was ready to try again. In less than a year, he scraped together enough money for the expedition. He found an old whaling ship called the *Terra Nova* and a crew of 65 men. But this time Scott had a rival, Roald Amundsen of Norway. The two men led separate expeditions to Antarctica. Their mission to reach the Pole became one of the most dramatic races of all time.

Captain Scott's ship *Terra Nova* set sail from Wales on June 15, 1910. This photograph shows the ship at Cape Evans in Antarctica.

The Earth's Poles

*The South Pole is the most southerly point on the surface of Earth. The **North Pole** is the northernmost point. The South Pole is found on the continent of Antarctica. The North Pole is in the middle of the **Arctic Ocean**, where the sea is mostly frozen over.*

Amundsen's idea

The Norwegian explorer Roald Amundsen was as determined as Scott to reach the South Pole. Amundsen had originally planned to become the first person to reach the *North* Pole. But in April 1909 the U.S. explorer Robert Peary got there first. Amundsen then decided to head to Antarctica and the South Pole instead.

Robert Peary made eight Arctic expeditions before finally conquering the North Pole in 1909. This painting shows Peary and his team at the Pole.

Until 1909 the British had explored more of Antarctica than any other nation. They believed this gave them the right over anyone else to explore the area further. But Amundsen did not agree. He said that he should be free to explore anywhere, declaring, "First come, first served is an old saying." Amundsen told nobody about his plans except his brother. He borrowed a ship called *Fram* and found a crew and dogs for the mission.

Surprise news

When Amundsen's expedition left Christiania (now Oslo, the capital city of Norway) in June 1910, only a handful of people knew where they were going. Amundsen told the crew in September, soon after a stop on the Spanish island of Madeira.

Scott had known about Amundsen's plans to discover the North Pole. But he did not find out the latest news until October, when he received a short telegram: "Beg leave to inform you *Fram* proceeding Antarctic. Amundsen." Now the race began. Both explorers wanted the honor of being the first person to reach the South Pole.

Scott's reaction

Scott showed how he felt about Amundsen's news in a letter to the Norwegian polar explorer Fridtjof Nansen:

"The fact that he departs with so much mystery leaves one with an uncomfortable feeling that he contemplates something which he imagines we should not approve."

Roald Amundsen

*Roald Engelbregt Gravning Amundsen (1872–1928) was born in Borge, Norway. He gave up medical school to try a life of adventure, including being part of the first team to spend a winter in Antarctica. Between 1902 and 1906, Amundsen crossed the **Northwest Passage** (a waterway north of Canada) and was the first person to sail it in both directions. Later, he flew an airship across the North Pole. Amundsen died in 1928, while on a rescue mission in the Arctic.*

This photograph of Roald Amundsen was taken in 1903.

The Contest Begins

Scott had a small headstart over Amundsen when the race to the **South Pole** began. His ship *Terra Nova* left New Zealand, the last stop before Antarctica, on November 29, 1910. But problems were in store for the British team.

A stormy ride

Terra Nova was weighed down with food, clothing, and medical supplies, as well as heavy scientific instruments, 3 motor sleds, 19 ponies, and 33 dogs. Two days after leaving New Zealand, the ship hit a terrible storm. Water gushed in and the engines failed. All men pumped out water as the powerful waves crashed onto deck. Both ship and crew were tested to their limits.

There were more dangers to come. For three weeks the ship was caught in **pack ice**. Scott just managed to control his bad temper. Then, on January 1, 1911, he sighted Mount Erebus—the volcano on Ross Island, Antarctica. On January 4 the British set up their base camp at a place they named Cape Evans.

A safe passage

Amundsen had a crew of 19 men and 116 dogs, and *Fram*'s load was much lighter than *Terra Nova*'s. The Norwegians passed easily through the storm that Scott had suffered. On January 15 they reached the Bay of Whales and set up their base camp, Framheim (meaning "Home of the *Fram*").

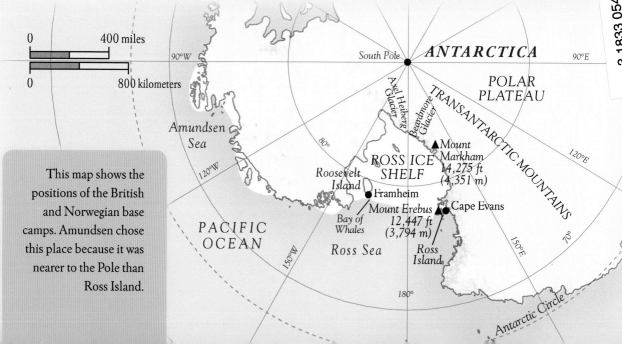

This map shows the positions of the British and Norwegian base camps. Amundsen chose this place because it was nearer to the Pole than Ross Island.

Antarctica's ice shelves

Both teams' base camps were near the edge of the Ross Ice Shelf, sometimes called the Great Ice Barrier. Ice shelves are floating masses of ice that surround the coastline of Antarctica. They are often connected to the land. The surface of the ice shelf is quite flat with gentle ripples. But where the ice shelf meets the land, there can be cracks or **crevasses**. Sea ice surrounding the ice shelf usually melts and breaks off in summer. The Ross Ice Shelf is the largest in Antarctica, covering about 302,425 square miles (487,000 square kilometers)—an area bigger than twice the size of Montana.

The Midnight Sun

Antarctica is known as the land of the Midnight Sun because during the Antarctic summer the Sun never sets. As Amundsen looked out at the bright, icy scenery, he wrote in his diary:

"There lies the barrier, probably as it lay thousands of years ago, bathed in the rays of the Midnight Sun."

This photograph shows a section of the Ross Ice Shelf. In some places the ice is several hundred feet thick. Most of the ice is below the surface of the sea.

Route to the Pole

Now that the teams were in Antarctica, the serious business of planning the trip to the South Pole could begin. Scott and Amundsen chose different routes, but they both had to trek across the Ross Ice Shelf, climb the Transantarctic Mountains, and pass the **Polar Plateau** to reach their goal.

In Shackleton's steps

In 1907–1909 the British explorer Ernest Shackleton had traveled across the Ross Ice Shelf and climbed the **Beardmore Glacier**. He set a new record by reaching a **latitude** of 88°23'S (see box below)—further south than anyone had been before. Scott aimed to follow Shackleton's route up the glacier. He also planned to use ponies, as Shackleton had done.

Members of Shackleton's party tend to their ponies on the British expedition of 1907–1909. Shackleton died in 1922 on his fourth visit to Antarctica.

Finding the South Pole

Scott and Amundsen used measurements called latitude and **longitude** to find their position. On maps these are marked as lines dividing Earth. Lines of latitude are horizontal. They show distance north and south of the **Equator**. Lines of longitude are vertical. They show distance east and west of the **Prime Meridian**. Measurements of latitude and longitude are made in degrees (°) and minutes ('), along with a direction: north, south, east, or west (N, S, E, W). The latitude of the South Pole is 90°S, while the **North Pole** is 90°N. Explorers can measure latitude and longitude using specialized equipment.

Taking a risk

Amundsen planned a new route across the Transantarctic Mountains. It was a risk, but his team was better prepared than Scott's. First, Framheim was 60 miles (96 kilometers) nearer to the South Pole than Scott's base camp. Also, the Norwegians were excellent skiers. Most of Scott's men had never used skis before.

The Transantarctic Mountains

The Transantarctic Mountains stretch for about 3,000 miles (4,800 kilometers) across Antarctica, dividing the continent's east and west. The mountains are mostly buried in snow, but there are some steep, rocky peaks. Some of the tallest peaks reach nearly 14,760 feet (4,500 meters) high. They form part of the Antarctic Polar Plateau, the highest land in Antarctica. This landscape would be a challenge to cross.

The Transantarctic mountain range is also called the TA Horst. Parts of the mountains still remain unexplored.

Preparing to Survive

The teams had little time to lose before the Antarctic weather turned harsh in March. Both expeditions needed to lay down **depots** (bases) containing food, fuel, and equipment along the route to the **South Pole**.

The British brought plenty of supplies with them to Cape Evans. Their hut was **insulated** with seaweed and lit by gas.

Extreme conditions

Antarctica has four seasons, but it feels like there are just two. During the summer months, from December to March, the Sun never sets and there is light 24 hours a day. But then the Sun begins to sink in the sky. The hours of daylight lessen, and by June there is 24-hour darkness. It stays this way until the Sun appears again in August. Arriving in Antarctica in mid-January gave the teams little time to prepare before the darkness of winter fell.

Ready for winter

Captain Scott planned an important depot at 80°S. It would be called One Ton Depot and would hold 1 ton (just over 1 tonne) of supplies. On January 24 the British sleds left to lay this depot and several others. A few days later, *Terra Nova* and a small crew set sail for New Zealand to avoid getting iced in during winter.

At Framheim, the Norwegians were busy hunting seals and penguins for meat. Roald Amundsen was pleased that everything was going according to plan. Then, on February 3, *Terra Nova* came across the camp on its way to New Zealand. The British were impressed with their Norwegian rivals' set-up, particularly the dogs. Husky dogs are strong, loyal animals. But they can be disobedient and need a firm master. The Norwegians knew how to handle them.

Beasts of burden

Scott believed that ponies would be able to carry heavier loads than dogs. He chose ponies from Manchuria (a mountainous area in northeastern China) because they were used to cold weather. Captain Oates took care of the ponies. He thought many of them were too old and weak. Ponies eat grass, so feeding them in Antarctica—the land of snow and ice—was a problem.

Seals swim in the icy Antarctic waters. The explorers ate fresh seal meat to give them vitamin C. A lack of vitamin C causes a disease called **scurvy**, which weakens sufferers and can kill if it goes untreated.

A test run

On February 10 Roald Amundsen left Framheim to lay some depots. Scott had the advantage this time because he was taking a known route. For Amundsen, this was a test run to find a good way across the Ross Ice Shelf. Like Scott, Amundsen planned a depot at 80°S.

The Norwegians made fast progress. They were expert skiers and they covered 15 miles (24 kilometers) in the first day. At noon they stopped for a cup of steaming hot chocolate served from a new invention called a thermos flask. The teams of dogs were also doing well, and two days later the Norwegians had raced for nearly 100 miles (160 kilometers). On February 14 they reached 80°S. They were back at base camp in two days. Amundsen was thrilled it had gone so smoothly, although he wished he had made it back in time to see *Fram* leave for winter. Amundsen now began planning another depot journey, aiming to reach 83°S.

This photograph shows one of the Norwegians' supply depots on the route to the Pole.

Scott doubts Amundsen

Scott did not have much faith in the Norwegians' team of dogs:

"As for Amundsen's prospects [chances] of reaching the Pole, I don't think they are very good. . . . I don't think he knows how bad an effect . . . the hard traveling surface of the Barrier [the Ice Shelf] is to animals."

Huskies enjoy working as a team, and there is always a leader of the pack. These dogs are pulling a sled for tourists in Greenland.

Scott's change of plan

The day the Norwegians arrived back at Framheim, the British were still struggling to reach 80°S. Somebody had forgotten to take the special snow shoes for the ponies. Without them, the animals' feet sank in the powdery snow. Eventually, Scott decided to base One Ton Camp at 79°29'S. This was about 31 miles (58 kilometers) short of his original plan.

Made for the cold

In addition to Scott's ponies, both the British and Norwegian teams used husky dogs. These dogs are closely related to wolves and can stand temperatures well below freezing— -58°F or -50°C is their limit. They have thick fur to keep them warm. At night they snuggle into the snow to insulate themselves against the cold. Huskies eat meat, so they can be fed penguins, seals, or even each other.

The Sun Goes Down

By the end of April 1911, winter darkness was falling over Antarctica. Both expeditions had laid their main **depots**. Now, they could settle at base camp and make final plans for their journeys.

Winter activities

Over the winter months there was plenty of time for mending and adapting equipment. The Norwegians made new boots because their fur ones had frozen badly during the depot journeys. The British worked on their ski boots and sleds. There were also hours to relax and enjoy the snow. Both teams skied and played moonlight soccer. Once a week, the Norwegians had a **sauna**. On June 22 there were midwinter celebrations. For the British at Cape Evans, it was like Christmas with a big meal and presents.

The coldest place on Earth

Antarctica is the coldest place on Earth. During winter, the average temperature is -76°F (-60°C). At Vostok, the Russian research station in Antarctica, scientists have noted temperatures as low as -132°F (-91°C). But the official record was registered at Vostok on July 21, 1983, when temperatures reached -128.6°F (-89.2°C).

Norwegian expedition members sew inside their base at Framheim during the winter of 1911.

A science mission

The British team was interested in science as well as exploring. The chief scientist was **zoologist** Dr. Edward Wilson. On June 27 Wilson and two others left camp for Cape Crozier, on the other side of Ross Island. They traveled west across the Ice Shelf on a journey expected to take five weeks. They hoped to bring back eggs from emperor penguins, to help them find out more about these birds. They were setting off in the dead dark of winter. Nobody had ever attempted to explore during an Antarctic winter before.

Emperor penguins

Antarctica is famous for its emperor penguins. In April the birds head to the south of the continent to nest. The female emperor penguin lays an egg in May, then heads to the sea to feed on fish during winter. Meanwhile, the male stays behind to protect the egg. Thousands of male penguins huddle together to keep warm. They each keep their egg in a special pouch between their feet. During this time they have no food to eat. The females return in July when the eggs have hatched. They then care for the chicks while the males go to the sea to fatten up.

Emperor penguin chicks huddle together to keep warm. When they grow up, these chicks can reach just under 4 feet (1.2 meters) tall.

"Worst journey in the world"

The British expedition to find the penguins at Cape Crozier was very hard. Traveling in the dark was difficult, and the weather was bitterly cold. By July, temperatures dipped to -76°F (-60°C). Part of the problem was the mens' clothing—it became sweaty when the walkers moved. At night the sweat froze and made the clothes heavier and colder. The mens' sleeping bags and tents more than doubled in weight from ice, too. The sleds grew heavier and heavier.

Antarctic skies

The winter journey was terrifying, but Wilson recorded some beautiful moments. He was impressed by the displays of swirling colors that he saw in the night sky. Patches of green, red, and violet lit up the darkness. This is called an **aurora** *(below). Auroras happen near both the* **South Pole** *and the* **North Pole**. *People in northern parts of Canada, Russia, and Scandinavia can see them on most clear winter nights.*

The remarkable aurora australis (the southern lights) light up the skies at the South Pole. At the North Pole they are called the aurora borealis (the northern lights).

During the following weeks, the men experienced **blizzards**, freezing thick fog, and icy Antarctic winds. One man's teeth split from the cold and another man fell through sea ice. When they finally reached the emperor penguins, they managed to collect three eggs. During the return journey the men lost their tent in a blizzard. Somehow they found the tent and survived the ordeal. They returned to camp thinner but wiser. The eggs proved useful for scientific research.

Lessons from Netsiliks

The British team's cotton and wool clothing did not always work well in Antarctica. Roald Amundsen learned how to dress in polar conditions from the Netsiliks, a group of Canadian **Inuit** people. They coped with the freezing weather by wearing several layers of clothing. Air trapped between the layers **insulated** them against the cold. Amundsen and his team used Netsilik reindeer clothing throughout the expedition. Sometimes they were too warm and the men stripped to their underclothes!

Katabatic winds

*Some of the strongest winds in the world blow in Antarctica. The most powerful blasts are called katabatic winds. These are formed when cold air from the **Polar Plateau** rushes down to the coast. At times the winds' speed can reach 200 miles per hour (320 kilometers per hour)—more than twice as fast as a hurricane-force wind.*

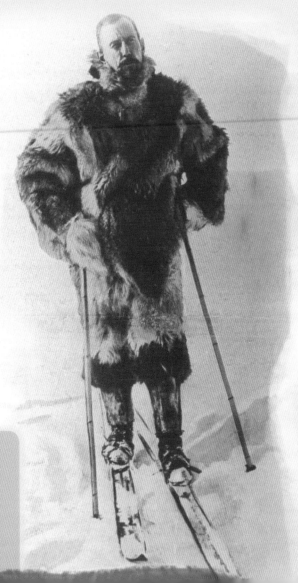

Roald Amundsen poses in his warm reindeer clothing. The British also used reindeer fur for sleeping bags.

Spring Starts the Race

The sunrise on August 24, 1911, was like the shot of a starting gun in a race. Spring was near, and Roald Amundsen was ready to go. His second in command, Hjalmar Johansen, was not so eager to hurry on.

A false start

Temperatures at the end of winter were still very low, around -40°F (-40°C). It was too cold for the dogs. Even Amundsen reported that his nostrils froze up. Nevertheless, on September 8, eight Norwegians set off for the **South Pole**. It was not an easy start. The dogs had been resting for six months and were difficult to control. On the first night the men shivered in their sleeping bags.

Conditions did not improve, so Amundsen finally decided to return to Framheim. Afterwards, some of the men stayed in bed nursing frostbitten feet for 10 days. The **frostbite** was painful, as was the feeling of disappointment. Five dogs also died on the mission. The men held back until October 20. Then, the Norwegian expedition set off for the South Pole again. This time the party included 5 men, 4 sleds, and 52 dogs.

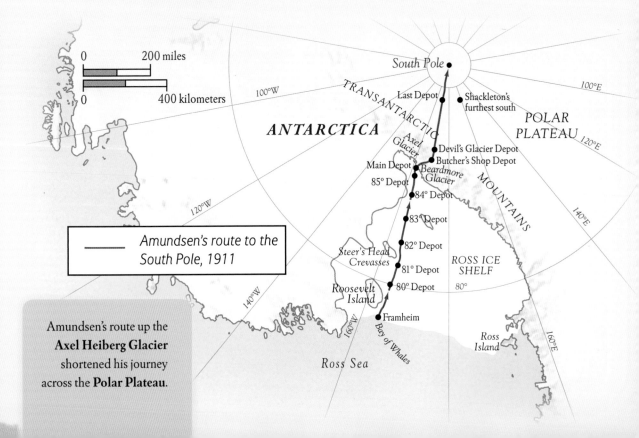

Amundsen's route up the **Axel Heiberg Glacier** shortened his journey across the **Polar Plateau**.

Frostbite

Being **exposed** to extreme cold can cause a dangerous condition called frostbite. Frostbitten skin becomes hard and pale. The area loses feeling, but there can be an aching pain. As the body warms up, the skin begins to **thaw** and soften. It gets red and is very painful. In bad cases the blood supply is cut off and **gangrene** can set in. Sometimes the only cure is to cut off the affected limb.

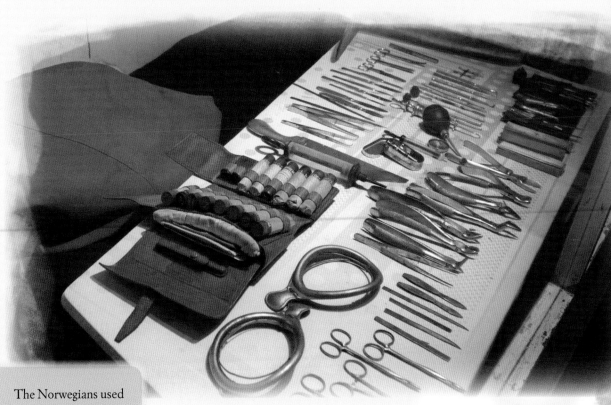

The Norwegians used these surgical instruments during their polar expedition. Both teams needed to be prepared for medical emergencies.

Expedition nerves

The Norwegian Olav Bjaaland described his fears as he set off for the second time to the South Pole:

"Now we are ready again. I hope it won't be a [failure] like the last time. . . . If I emerge [unharmed] from this journey, I must see that I get out of polar exploration."

Anxious to leave

By October, Captain Robert Scott was moody and anxious to set off, too. The ponies held him back. These animals could not handle extreme cold. When they pulled the sleds, they would sweat. Later, the sweat turned into a freezing layer of ice. Scott was also having bad dreams. During one nightmare his son Peter told him, "Daddy, you won't come back."

The British plan

The British polar party was made up of 16 men, 10 ponies, 33 dogs, 2 motorized sleds, and 13 wooden sleds. Scott divided them into four teams. Only one team would go all the way to the South Pole. The others were there to help carry supplies and would turn back at various stages. Scott hoped the ponies would make it across the Ross Ice Shelf. They would be shot and eaten when they became too tired. The dogs should reach the bottom of the **Beardmore Glacier**. From there, the five strongest men would pull the sleds all the way to the South Pole.

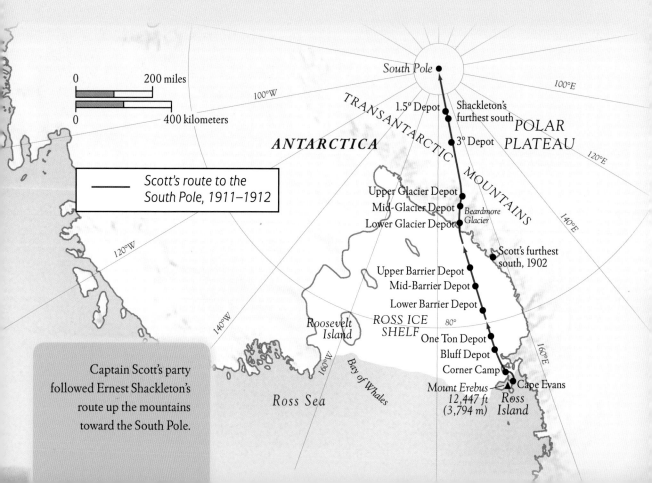

Captain Scott's party followed Ernest Shackleton's route up the mountains toward the South Pole.

On October 24, 1911, the first team rolled out of Cape Evans with the two motorized sleds. On November 1 the sleds broke down. That same date, Scott led the other teams out onto the Ice Shelf. They were 12 days behind Amundsen's second start.

The first snowmobiles

Scott's motorized sleds were ahead of their time. They were used as an experiment and did the job better than expected. They covered 51 miles (82 kilometers) on the journey before they broke down. Their design has since been important to creators of army tanks and the snowmobiles that are used in Antarctica today.

The British used the first motorized sleds in Antarctica. The sleds worked well on the ice because they had tracks rather than wheels.

A matter of equipment

Captain Oates wrote to his mother about the competition with the Norwegians:

"I expect they have started for the Pole ... and have a jolly good chance of getting there if their dogs are good and they use them properly. From what I see I think it would not be difficult to get to the Pole provided you have proper transport but with the rubbish [poor equipment] we have it will be jolly difficult and mean a lot of hard work."

Journey Across the Ice

The Norwegians made good progress across the Ice Shelf. The dogs began to behave and the men skied 15–20 miles (24–32 kilometers) a day. Scott's expedition struggled on, too. However, both teams would run into problems.

A step away from death

Amundsen and his men were not scared away by "pea-souper" fog (fog so thick it looks like soup) or raging **blizzards**. But they were crossing unknown land. Sooner or later they were bound to hit something unexpected.

On November 1 Amundsen stumbled into a field of **crevasses** (see box on the far right). Today, this area, called Steer's Head crevasses, is a well-known danger spot. Two men nearly fell to their death. The going was tough, but on November 4 the Norwegians reached the last **depot** where they had left supplies. They picked up enough food and fuel to get them to the Pole and back. The **South Pole** lay just over 480 miles (772 kilometers) away.

Scott's team

Captain Scott's men had trouble of their own. On the Ice Shelf, the weather turned against them. Snow fell without stopping. Icy winds blasted the snow into everyone's faces and damaged the ponies' eyes. The men tried to use skis, but had to give up because they scared the ponies. The team battled on, managing about 12 miles (19 kilometers) a day. They mostly traveled by night to avoid white-outs (see box on the right).

What is a white-out?

*One of the most dangerous times to travel on the Ice Shelf is during a white-out. This is when the sky is white or thick with clouds. The sky blends in with the snow-covered ground and the **horizon** disappears from view. Explorers can quickly get lost in white-outs. Scott chose to travel at night because the dark sky made it easier to see where the sky finished and the ground began.*

Danger lies below.
A skier carefully
crosses a huge crevasse.
A mistake could cost
him his life.

Crevasses

A crevasse is a deep crack
in the ice. The crack can
be anything from a few
millimeters to about
100 feet (30 meters) wide.
Big crevasses are dangerous
because they are usually
covered with snow. The best
way to cross them is to find
a place where the snow
is thick and has formed a
snow bridge. In Antarctica
most crevasses are near the
Transantarctic Mountains.

Amundsen on top

On November 15 Roald Amundsen reached the foot of a gigantic glacier. A glacier is a massive stretch of ice and snow that usually moves from high ground slowly downward toward the sea. As the glacier moves, it erodes (wears away) the landscape and carves out shapes such as valleys. The Lambert Glacier in Antarctica is thought to be the largest in the world.

Amundsen had arrived at the **Axel Heiberg Glacier**. Nobody had ever climbed it before, so the team did not know what to expect. Scott had doubted that dogs with sleds would make it up the mountains. Amundsen proved him wrong by taking his full team of dogs to the top. It took just six days. Soon afterward, 24 of the dogs were shot and fed to the other animals.

This photograph shows the ice cliffs of the Barne Glacier in Antarctica.

British behind

Scott reached One Ton Depot on November 15. He checked his progress against Shackleton's journey of 1908. His team was six days behind Shackleton's times. On November 21 the main party set off toward the **Beardmore Glacier**. A few days later a first team headed back to Cape Evans. A pony was killed for meat, and the hungry dogs gobbled it up. The men made a tasty stew of crackers, raisins, curry paste, cocoa, and half-raw pony meat.

Captain Scott, Evans, Bowers, and Wilson warm up with hot drinks and food. The team used stoves lit with blubber oil from seals.

Weather watch

Why did Scott experience bad weather when Amundsen was climbing in clear blue skies? Being on higher ground helped Amundsen. In mountain regions, winds often blow from the bottom of a slope upward. They may carry snow and fog with them. The winds can run out of steam as they push up the mountains, so the bad weather does not always reach higher up.

Held up again

On November 29, after weeks on the Ice Shelf, Scott saw Mount Markham in the distance. The Beardmore Glacier was within reach. Everyone felt excited—but a few days later the weather turned bad. A terrible storm kept the men trapped in their tents for four days, losing more precious time.

The British began climbing the Beardmore Glacier on December 9. They shot the last pony and sent the dogs back to Cape Evans. Now, there were three teams of four men pulling sleds up the mountain.

Getting weaker

Conditions were difficult. The sleds sank in the deep, soft snow. To make matters worse, some men had snow blindness (see box above right). Everyone was getting weaker, but no one complained out loud—if they admitted to weakness, they would not be picked to go all the way to the Pole. Bowers was the strongest, but even he struggled with the sled harness. He wrote that it "nearly crushed my insides into my backbone by the everlasting jerking with all one's strength on the canvas bound round my unfortunate tummy."

The British pause for a moment on the Beardmore Glacier. They could not stop for long because their sweat would have frozen in the extreme cold.

Snow blindness
Snow blindness is a common problem for explorers in the polar regions. It happens when the snow reflects glaring sunlight into a person's eyes. The eyes become sore, red, and difficult to open, as if they are sunburned. Wearing sunglasses or goggles helps to prevent snow blindness. The only cure is to rest the eyes in a darkened room.

Modern explorers have better clothes and equipment to protect them from the cold. These goggles filter out harmful rays of sunshine.

A high-energy diet

In the extreme cold, people need more food and **nutrients** to survive. Both expeditions took a special diet that was light to carry. The Norwegians ate high-energy crackers, pemmican, chocolate, and milk powder. The British ate similar crackers, pemmican, butter, cocoa, sugar, and tea. Pemmican is a cake made of dried meat and melted fat. Along with the crackers and chocolate, this gave the men energy. The milk powder provided calcium for strong bones. At the depots the men also picked up frozen meat to eat. This contained vitamin C, which they needed to fight off illness, especially **scurvy**.

Approaching the Pole

Traveling across the **Polar Plateau** was hard work, but the Norwegians battled on through **blizzards** and fog. By December they had made good ground. Their goal was not far off.

Close to the mark

On December 8 Roald Amundsen reached 88°23'S—the record set by Ernest Shackleton (see page 12). Everybody ate extra chocolate to celebrate. They had about 95 miles (153 kilometers) to go before they reached the **South Pole**.

The weather was good. The sleds and skis flew over the hard snow.

On the evening of December 13, the Norwegians camped just 15 miles (24 kilometers) from the South Pole. Everybody was excited and nervous. Perhaps Captain Robert Scott *had* won the race. They did not know. The next morning they set off quickly. All eyes were fixed on the **horizon**. As they got closer to the Pole, they were excited. There was no British flag to be seen.

First to the Pole

At 3:00 p.m. on December 14, the explorers shouted, "Halt!" They had reached 90°S. Amundsen went ahead to become the first person to set foot at the South Pole. Then, the men stuck the Norwegian flag in the ground together. Amundsen spoke: "So we plant you, dear flag, on the South Pole, and give the plain on which it lies the name King Haakon VII's Plateau."

The Norwegians marked the South Pole with their flag. Amundsen named the camp Polheim, "Home of the Pole."

Joint effort

Amundsen explained why he wanted the whole team to plant the flag at the South Pole:

"I had decided that we would all take part in the historic event; the act itself of planting the flag. It was not the privilege [honor or right] of one man, it was the privilege of all those who had risked their lives in the fight and stood together through thick and thin."

The Amundsen-Scott South Pole Station

There was no permanent building at the South Pole until 1957. Then, the United States built an international research base there. It was named the Amundsen-Scott South Pole Station. Since then the station has had to be rebuilt twice because of the build-up of snow. Today's station is raised above the ground on stilts to prevent it from being buried by snow. It is about 330 feet (100 meters) from the South Pole and is used mainly by scientists (see page 40).

The Amundsen-Scott South Pole Station was rebuilt in 2003.

"Farewell dear Pole"

The day after the Norwegians had marked their victory, Roald Amundsen got up early. He wanted to be certain that they had reached the exact South Pole. The men used a tool called a **sextant** to make detailed calculations of their **latitude** and **longitude**. After three days they found the exact point of 90°S. The explorers built a small tent there and put equipment and clothing inside. Amundsen also left letters for the king of Norway and Captain Scott. He asked Scott to forward the letter to the king if Amundsen died. On December 17 the Norwegians packed up and left. Amundsen wrote in his diary: "Farewell dear Pole, I don't think we'll meet again."

Roald Amundsen, Helmer Hanssen, Sverre Hassel, and Oscar Wisting bid farewell to the tent at the South Pole.

Team for the top

On January 3, 1912, Captain Robert Scott finally reached the top of the **Beardmore Glacier**. He announced his final team. It was himself, Captain Lawrence Oates, Edgar Evans, Dr. Edward Wilson, and Lieutenant Henry Bowers. The others were to head back to camp as planned. They were 150 miles (241 kilometers) away from the South Pole.

"Let's leg it," Scott told his men when he wanted them to push themselves. But soon everyone was exhausted. The rations did not fill them up. They were also showing signs of **scurvy**. On January 9 the British passed Shackleton's furthest-south record. There was still no sign of the Norwegians.

Then, temperatures dipped. Sharp crystals formed on the ice, making it difficult to pull the sleds. The men also had to deal with fields of **sastrugi**. Some days the team covered only 5 miles (8 kilometers). On January 16 they expected to reach the Pole the next day. At 4:00 p.m. Bowers spotted something in the distance. Was it a cairn? (See box on the right.) The men hoped their eyes were fooling them. A cairn would mean the Norwegians had gotten there first.

What is a cairn?
A cairn is like a marker in the snow. It is built from a pile of stones. Explorers make cairns to show the position of a camp, base, or burial site. Cairns can be seen from many miles away in the snow.

A field of sastrugi dominates this landscape at Cape Norvegia in Antarctica. Sastrugi are wind-blown shapes in the snow. They can be frozen hard as concrete and stand several feet high, making them very difficult for explorers to pass.

Journey's End

On January 17 Captain Robert Scott and his team finally reached the **South Pole**. The next day they found the Norwegians' tent. They read Roald Amundsen's letter and discovered that the Norwegians had been there a month earlier.

Captain Scott and his team inspect the Norwegian tent at the South Pole. In addition to letters, they found equipment left for them by the Norwegians.

"A Desperate Struggle"

Scott wrote in his diary: "Great God! This is an awful place and terrible enough for us to have labored to it without the reward of [getting here first]." The next day the British began their homeward journey. Scott wrote in his diary again: "Now for the run home and a desperate struggle. I wonder if we can do it."

For three weeks the men made good time. On February 4 Evans fell down a **crevasse**, hit his head, and got a **concussion**. He kept going, but each step was a struggle. As the days went by, he became silent and gloomy. His nose was badly affected by **frostbite** and looked rotten.

Heavy science

Even when the going was tough, the British team collected scientific information. The rock samples they gathered on the journey weighed about 35 pounds (15 kilograms). This made the sleds even heavier. Some critics say they should have dumped the rocks and fossils to lighten the load.

The British suffered greatly because they pulled their equipment themselves for most of the journey. On the final leg of the expedition, they were exhausted.

Amundsen returns

While the British team struggled, Roald Amundsen and his men were on the home stretch. For a while they got lost and could not find the next **depot**. They were in danger of running out of dog food. On January 5 they finally found their depot and began their climb down the **Axel Heiberg Glacier**. On January 6 they were back on the Ice Shelf. For the first time, the men really felt the cold. They made it back to Framheim on January 26, 1912.

Celebrations

One of the Norwegians, Oscar Wisting, recalled the first morning back at Framheim:

"Have you been there?' 'Yes, we've been there,' answered Roald Amundsen, and then there was a hullabaloo [uproar]. Soon after, we were all seated around the table and savored Lindstrom's [the cook at Framheim] hot cakes and heavenly coffee. How good a cup of coffee can really taste one only realizes when, like us, one has had to go without so long."

Dying men

The British plodded onward. They still had more than 400 miles (640 kilometers) to go, and Edgar Evans was slowing them down. On February 17, at the bottom of the **Beardmore Glacier**, Evans collapsed and died. There was no time to bury him. The team did not know what had killed him. Historians think it could have been **scurvy**, starvation, or the fall and blow to his head.

Winter brought temperatures of -40°F (-40°C). Captain Lawrence Oates had a badly frostbitten foot. By March 6 he was too weak to pull the sled. Oates struggled on, but on March 16 he asked the others to leave him. They refused. That night in the tent during a **blizzard**, Oates told them: "I am just going outside and may be some time." He walked out and was never seen again.

Freak weather

Scott and his party suffered some of the coldest weather ever recorded for that time of year in Antarctica. The March temperatures noted in Scott's diary were up to 20°F (11°C) colder than average figures.

Final days

The end was not far away for Captain Robert Scott, Dr. Edward Wilson, and Lieutenant Henry Bowers. Two days later they made their final camp. They were 11 miles (17.7 kilometers) from One Ton Depot and safety. A blizzard trapped them in their tent. By now Scott had frostbite in his feet and could not move. Starving and exhausted, the men waited for death. They wrote letters to their families, and Scott composed a message to the public. He made his last diary entry on March 29, 1912: "Outside the door of the tent it remains a scene of whirling drift. I do not think we can hope for any better things now."

Brave farewell

Scott's "Message to the Public" was found in the tent with his body. In it, he wrote:

"Had we lived, I should have had a tale to tell of the hardihood, endurance, and courage of my companions which would have stirred the heart of every Englishman. These rough notes and our dead bodies must tell the tale."

This memorial cross was erected at Observation Hill in memory of Scott and the British party.

Every One a Hero?

On March 8, 1912, news of Amundsen's triumph spread around the world. His victory in the race to the **South Pole** was headline news. In Norway people hung out flags to celebrate. Americans regarded Amundsen as a hero, and President Theodore Roosevelt sent a telegram to congratulate him.

The success story

Amundsen was praised for his careful planning. He had made more **depots** than Scott, and he marked them clearly so they were easy to find. The Norwegians were expert skiers and used dogs instead of ponies. Amundsen also knew how to dress properly in polar conditions, having learned from the Netsilik people. Today, we know more about the importance of diet and vitamins. At Framheim, the Norwegians ate a well-balanced diet. They were fit for their journey to the Pole. And, once they were on that journey, they always had plenty of food.

Risky business

At first the tragic story of Captain Scott touched people's hearts. For many years he was considered a hero, too. Later, some historians criticized Scott for taking risks. One of his greatest mistakes was the position of One Ton Depot. It was 31.5 miles (58 kilometers) further from the Pole than he had planned. Perhaps this cost Scott and his men their lives. Some historians have praised Scott's team for being the first people to haul sleds to the South Pole.

Scientists in Antarctica

Today, there are research stations all over Antarctica, including the Amundsen-Scott South Pole Station (see page 33). Some of the stations are the size of small towns, with hundreds of people living and working there. Scientists study everything from the climate, dry land, seas, and lakes to plant life, animals, and birds. The first child was born on the Antarctic mainland in 1978, at an Argentine scientific base. Now, several children live and go to school there.

Global warming

Today, we know that the average temperature of Earth is slowly rising. This is called global warming, and it is changing the planet. In Antarctica, scientists are measuring the size of glaciers. In recent years the glaciers have been shrinking, which may be connected to global warming. Melting glaciers, flowing into the sea, might be a serious problem in the future. Rising sea levels could cause severe floods, swamping land and even wiping out whole communities.

These scientists in modern-day Antarctica are measuring the thickness of the ice using a weighted line.

Routes to the South Pole

This map shows the routes both explorers took in their race to the **South Pole**. They traveled from their home countries to Antarctica by sea.

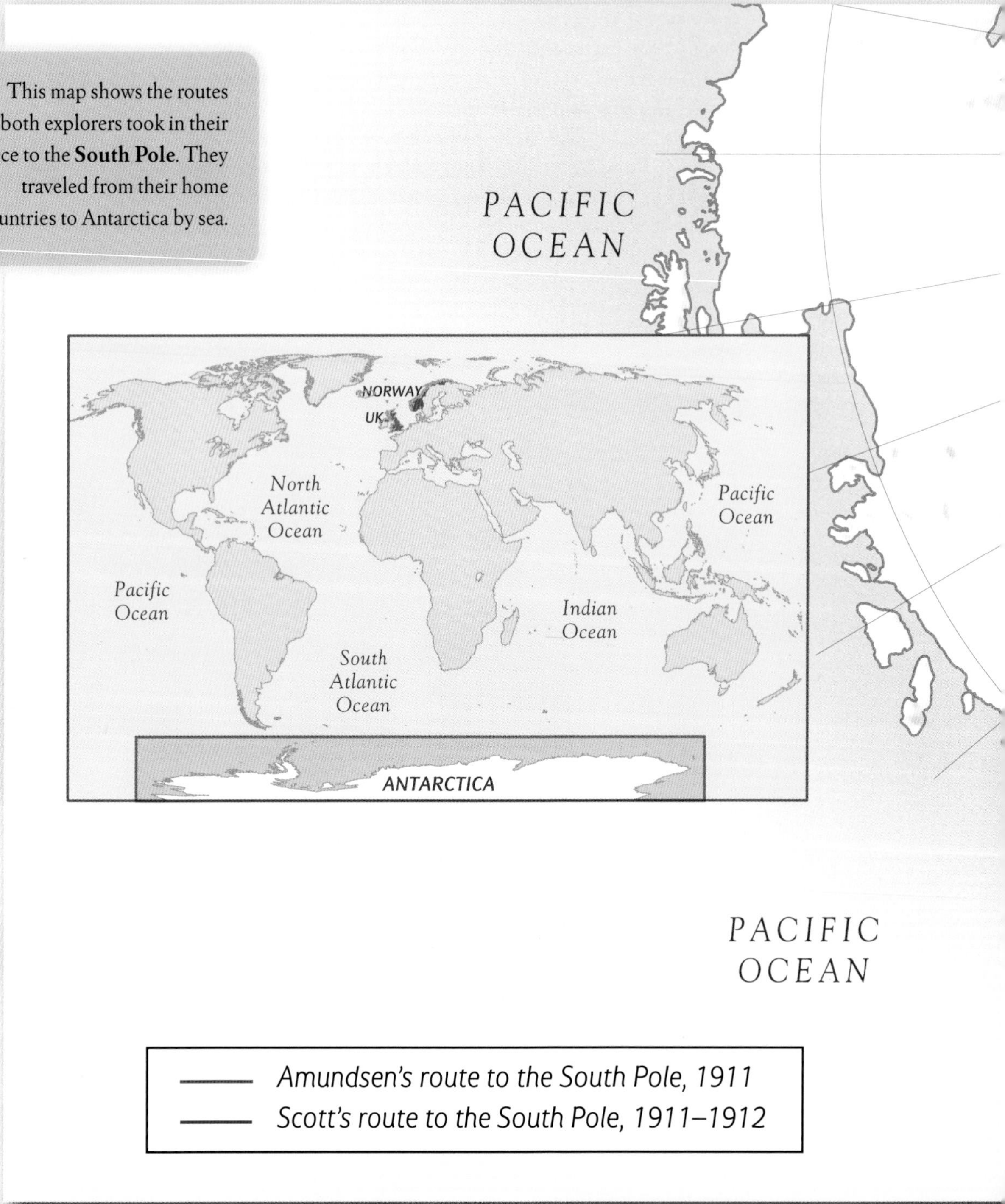

PACIFIC
OCEAN

NORWAY
UK

North
Atlantic
Ocean

Pacific
Ocean

Pacific
Ocean

Indian
Ocean

South
Atlantic
Ocean

ANTARCTICA

PACIFIC
OCEAN

——— Amundsen's route to the South Pole, 1911
——— Scott's route to the South Pole, 1911–1912

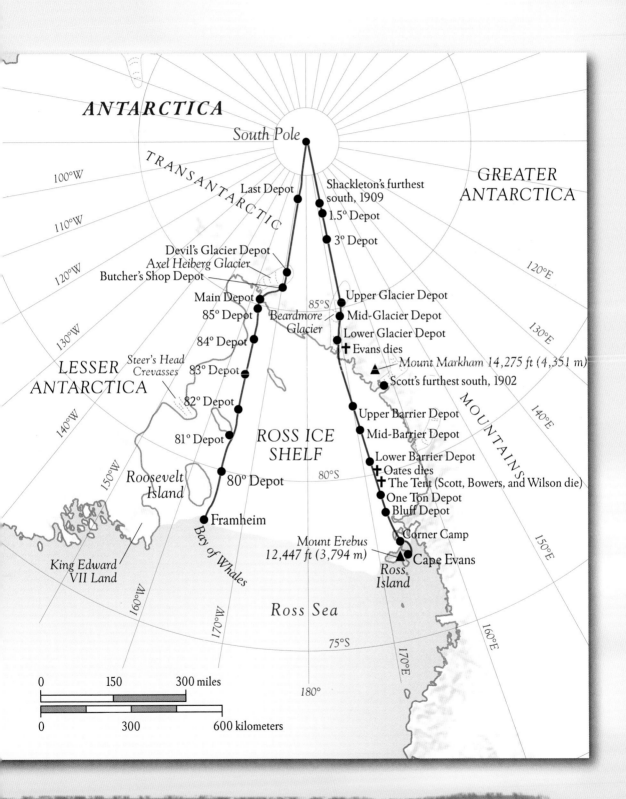

ANTARCTICA

South Pole

100°W

110°W

TRANSANTARCTIC

Last Depot

Shackleton's furthest
south, 1909

1.5° Depot

3° Depot

GREATER
ANTARCTICA

120°W

Devil's Glacier Depot
Axel Heiberg Glacier
Butcher's Shop Depot

120°E

130°W

Main Depot

85°S

Upper Glacier Depot

85° Depot

Beardmore
Glacier

Mid-Glacier Depot

130°E

84° Depot

Lower Glacier Depot

✝ Evans dies

LESSER
ANTARCTICA

Steer's Head
Crevasses

83° Depot

▲ Mount Markham 14,275 ft (4,351 m)

Scott's furthest south, 1902

82° Depot

140°W

81° Depot

ROSS ICE
SHELF

Upper Barrier Depot

Mid-Barrier Depot

140°E

MOUNTAINS

80° Depot

80°S

Lower Barrier Depot
✝ Oates dies
✝ The Tent (Scott, Bowers, and Wilson die)
One Ton Depot
Bluff Depot

150°W

Roosevelt
Island

Framheim

Corner Camp

150°E

King Edward
VII Land

160°W

Bay of Whales

170°W

Mount Erebus
12,447 ft (3,794 m)

Ross
Island

▲ Cape Evans

Ross Sea

75°S

170°E

160°E

180°

0   150   300 miles

0   300   600 kilometers

Timeline

June 6, 1868	Robert Falcon Scott is born in Devonport, near Plymouth, England.
July 16, 1872	Roald Amundsen is born at Borge near Christiania (now Oslo), Norway.
January 1898	Amundsen is the first person to ski in Antarctica; a few days later he heads the first sledding expedition there.
July 1901	Scott heads his first British Antarctic Expedition.
January 1902	Scott crosses the Antarctic Circle and sights Antarctica for the first time.
February 1902	Scott flies the first balloon over Antarctica at the Bay of Whales.
November 1902	Scott, Ernest Shackleton, and Edward Wilson make a first attempt to reach the **South Pole.**
December 1902	Scott reaches 82°17'S and sets the record for the farthest south.
January 1909	Ernest Shackleton reaches 88°38'S and sets a new record.
June 1910	Scott leaves Great Britain on his second polar journey, aboard *Terra Nova.*
June 1910	Amundsen's ship *Fram* leaves Christiania, Norway.
January 2, 1911	Scott arrives in Antarctica and makes a base at Cape Evans.
January 15, 1911	Amundsen arrives in Antarctica, making a base called Framheim.
September 8, 1911	Amundsen sets off on his first attempt to reach the South Pole, but turns back after a week because of cold weather.
October 20, 1911	Amundsen sets off again on his second attempt to reach the South Pole.
November 1, 1911	Scott sets out from Cape Evans toward the South Pole.
December 14, 1911	Amundsen reaches the South Pole.
January 3, 1912	Scott announces the final team that will travel with him to the South Pole.
January 17, 1912	Scott reaches the South Pole.

January 26, 1912	Amundsen returns to Framheim. A few days later he boards *Fram* and heads to New Zealand.
March 8, 1912	Amundsen announces his victory to the world via telegram.
March 29, 1912	Probable date of Scott, Wilson, and Bowers' death on the Ice Shelf.
November 12, 1912	A search party discovers the bodies of Scott, Wilson, and Bowers.
June 1928	Amundsen is killed during a rescue mission in the **Arctic.**
1947	Richard Byrd (United States) flies over the South Pole from the Ross Ice Shelf.
1956	John Torbert (United States) flies across Antarctica over the South Pole (Ross Island to Weddell Sea) and returns without landing.
October 1956	Conrad Shinn (United States) lands his plane at the South Pole, and a permanent station is established at the South Pole.
1958	Vivian Fuchs (Great Britain) reaches the South Pole with motor vehicles and sled dogs, then crosses Antarctica (Weddell Sea to Ross Sea).
January 1975	The Amundsen-Scott South Pole Station is dedicated to the two men.
1981	Sir Ranulph Fiennes (Great Britain) leads the Transglobe Expedition. He pulls sleds across Antarctica and arrives at Scott Base.
1990	The International Trans-Antarctic Expedition, led by Will Steger (United States) and Jean-Louis Etienne (France), crosses Antarctica using skis and dogs.
1993	The American Women's Expedition (AWE), led by Ann Bancroft (United States), skis to the South Pole.
1996	Borge Ousland (Norway) becomes the first person to cross Antarctica alone.

Glossary

Arctic belonging or relating to the north polar region

aurora colorful display of lights in the skies above the South and North Poles

Axel Heiberg Glacier glacier in Antarctica, flowing between the Herbert Range and Mount Don Pedro Christophersen in the Queen Maud Mountains

Beardmore Glacier glacier in Antarctica, flowing from the Queen Maud Mountains to the Ross Ice Shelf

blizzard severe snowstorm with high winds

concussion injury to the brain—often knocking a person out—that is caused by a blow to the head

crevasse deep crack in ice, especially in a glacier

depot site for storing food and equipment in the race to the South Pole

Equator imaginary line around Earth, at equal distance from the North and South Poles, found at latitude 0°

exposed uncovered and unprotected from the weather

frostbite injury caused by extreme cold. Skin of the ears, fingers, and toes may suffer from frostbite if exposed to freezing temperatures.

gangrene rotting or dying flesh because the blood supply has been cut off

horizon line where the sky seems to meet the land or sea

insulated designed to stop heat from escaping

Inuit group of Eskimo people, mostly living in Canada

latitude position of a place, measured in degrees north or south of the Equator

longitude position of a place, measured in degrees east or west of the Prime Meridian

North Pole point at the far north of Earth, in the freezing Arctic region

Northwest Passage sea passage along the northern coast of the North American continent, through the Canadian Arctic. The passage joins the Atlantic Ocean to the Pacific.

nutrient substance found in food and drink that helps the body to stay healthy

pack ice large pieces of floating ice that form a cover over large areas of sea

Polar Plateau area of high land in the mountains of Antarctica

Prime Meridian line of 0° longitude, passing through the Royal Greenwich Observatory in London, England. It is also known as the International Meridian or the Greenwich Meridian.

Royal Geographical Society (RGS) group set up in London, England, in 1830. The RGS supports exploration, learning, and research in geography.

sastrugi sculptured shapes in the snow, formed by wind-blown blizzards. Giant sastrugi are serious obstacles to explorers in Antarctica.

sauna type of steam bath, originally from Finland. Water is thrown onto hot coals to produce steam.

scurvy disease caused by a lack of vitamin C in the diet. Vitamin C is found in fresh fruits and vegetables and also in seal meat.

sextant scientific instrument used to find latitude and longitude based on the position of the Sun, stars, or Moon above the horizon

South Pole point at the far south of Earth, on the continent of Antarctica

thaw become soft or liquid after being frozen. Snow and ice thaw (melt) when the weather becomes warmer.

zoologist scientist who studies different species (types) of animals

Further Information

Books

Currie, Stephen. *Exploration and Discovery: Antarctica.* San Diego: Lucent, 2004.
A good history of exploration in Antarctica, from ancient Greek theories about the land through Byrd's explorations in the first half of the 20th century.

Green, Jen. *You Wouldn't Want to Be a Polar Explorer!: An Expedition You'd Rather Not Go On.* New York: Franklin Watts, 2001.
A very lively description of Ernest Shackleton's expedition to Antarctica, detailing all the dangers an Arctic explorer should look out for.

Karner, Julie. *Roald Amundsen: The Conquest of the South Pole.* New York: Crabtree, 2006.
Learn more details about Amundsen's expedition.

Reid, Greg. *Exploration: Antarctica.* North Mankato, Minn.: Chrysalis, 2005.
A good source for pictures and maps of Antarctica.

Websites

www.antarcticaonline.com/antarctica/home/home.htm
Learn about all aspects of Antarctica at this site, which includes sections on science, history (including expeditions), culture, and more.

www.antarcticconnection.com/antarctic/history/pole-race.shtml
A useful site that includes the story of the race to the South Pole as well as details on Antarctic weather, animals, history, and up-to-date news of what is going on in the region today.

www.south-pole.com/p0000101.htm
Learn more about the Norwegian explorer Roald Amundsen on this site. It includes good archive photography.

www.south-pole.com/p0000090.htm
A page dedicated to the life of Captain Robert Scott and his attempt to reach the South Pole. It includes excellent archive photography.

Places to Visit

National Museum of Natural History
Smithsonian Institution
Washington, D.C. 20013-7012
Phone: (202) 633-1000
Website: www.mnh.si.edu

The National Museum of Natural History's Arctic Studies Center studies the history and culture of the region. The Smithsonian has one of the world's finest collections of artifacts from Arctic regions.

Carnegie Museum of Natural History
4400 Forbes Avenue
Pittsburgh, Pennsylvania 15213
Phone: (412) 622-3131
Website: www.carnegiemnh.com

Visit Polar World: The Wyckoff Hall of Arctic Life at the Carnegie Museum of Natural History. This permanent exhibition features field equipment used by early expeditions, photographs from several expeditions, specimens from nature, and Inuit sculpture and prints.

Index